The Story of
RUBY BRIDGES

The Story of
RUBY BRIDGES

by ROBERT COLES
Illustrated by GEORGE FORD

SCHOLASTIC
HARDCOVER

SCHOLASTIC INC.
NEW YORK

To RUBY BRIDGES HALL
and to all who did as she did
for the United States of America
— R . C .

To my wife, BERNETTE,
who relived Ruby's ordeal with me
— G . F .

Library of Congress Cataloging-in-Publication Data

Coles, Robert.
The story of Ruby Bridges / by Robert Coles;
illustrated by George Ford.
p. cm.
Summary: For months, six-year-old Ruby Bridges
must confront the hostility of segregationists
when she becomes the first African-American girl to integrate
Frantz Elementary School in New Orleans in 1960.
ISBN 0-590-43967-7
1. Bridges, Ruby — Juvenile literature.
2. School integration — Louisiana — New Orleans — Juvenile literature.
3. New Orleans (La.) — Race relations — Juvenile literature.
4. Afro-Americans — Louisiana — New Orleans — Biography — Juvenile literature.
[1. School integration — Louisiana — New Orleans.
2. Bridges, Ruby. 3. Afro-Americans — Biography.
4. New Orleans (La.) — Race relations.]
I. Ford, George Cephas, ill. II. Title.
F379.N59N33 1995
370.19'342—dc20   92-33674
CIP
AC

12 11 10 9 8 7 6 5 4 3 2   5 6 7 8 9/9 0/0
Printed in the U.S.A.   36
First printing, February 1995
Designed by Marijka Kostiw

George Ford used watercolor paints mixed with
acrylic inks and conventional drawing inks
to create the illustrations for this book.

Our Ruby taught us all a lot.
She became someone who helped change our country.
She was part of history,
just like generals and presidents are part of history.
They're leaders, and so was Ruby.
She led us away from hate, and she led us nearer to
knowing each other,
the white folks and the black folks.

— RUBY'S MOTHER

Ruby Bridges was born in a small cabin near Tylerton, Mississippi. "We were very poor, very, very poor," Ruby said. "My daddy worked picking crops. We just barely got by. There were times when we didn't have much to eat. The people who owned the land were bringing in machines to pick the crops, so my daddy lost his job, and that's when we had to move. I remember us leaving. I was four, I think."

In 1957, the family moved to New Orleans. Ruby's father became a janitor. Her mother took care of the children during the day. After they were tucked in bed, Ruby's mother went to work scrubbing floors in a bank.

Every Sunday, the family went to church.

"We wanted our children to be near God's spirit," Ruby's mother said. "We wanted them to start feeling close to Him from the very start."

At that time, black children and white children went to separate schools in New Orleans. The black children were not able to receive the same education as the white children. It wasn't fair. And it was against the nation's law.

In 1960, a judge ordered four black girls to go to two white elementary schools. Three of the girls were sent to McDonogh 19. Six-year-old Ruby Bridges was sent to first grade in the William Frantz Elementary School.

Ruby's parents were proud that their daughter had been chosen to take part in an important event in American history. They went to church.

"We sat there and prayed to God," Ruby's mother said, "that we'd all be strong and we'd have courage and we'd get through any trouble; and Ruby would be a good girl and she'd hold her head up high and be a credit to her own people and a credit to all the American people. We prayed long and we prayed hard."

On Ruby's first day, a large crowd of angry white people gathered outside the Frantz Elementary School. The people carried signs that said they didn't want black children in a white school. People called Ruby names; some wanted to hurt her. The city and state police did not help Ruby.

The President of the United States ordered federal marshals to walk with Ruby into the school building. The marshals carried guns.

Every day, for weeks that turned into months, Ruby experienced that kind of school day.

She walked to the Frantz School surrounded by marshals. Wearing a clean dress and a bow in her hair and carrying her lunch pail, Ruby walked slowly for the first few blocks. As Ruby approached the school, she saw a crowd of people marching up and down the street. Men and women and children shouted at her. They pushed toward her. The marshals kept them from Ruby by threatening to arrest them.

Ruby would hurry through the crowd and not say a word.

The white people in the neighborhood would not send their children to school. When Ruby got inside the building, she was all alone except for her teacher, Miss Hurley. There were no other children to keep Ruby company, to play with and learn with, to eat lunch with.

But every day, Ruby went into the classroom with a big smile on her face, ready to get down to the business of learning.

"She was polite and she worked well at her desk," Miss Hurley said. "She enjoyed her time there. She didn't seem nervous or anxious or irritable or scared. She seemed as normal and relaxed as any child I've ever taught."

So Ruby began learning how to read and write in an empty classroom, an empty building.

"Sometimes I'd look at her and wonder how she did it," said Miss Hurley. "How she went by those mobs and sat here all by herself and yet seemed so relaxed and comfortable."

Miss Hurley would question Ruby in order to find out if the girl was really nervous and afraid even though she seemed so calm and confident. But Ruby kept saying she was doing fine.

The teacher decided to wait and see if Ruby would keep on being so relaxed and hopeful or if she'd gradually begin to wear down — or even decide that she no longer wanted to go to school.

Then one morning, something happened. Miss Hurley stood by a window in her classroom as she usually did, watching Ruby walk toward the school. Suddenly, Ruby stopped — right in front of the mob of howling and screaming people. She stood there facing all those men and women. She seemed to be talking to them.

Miss Hurley saw Ruby's lips moving and wondered what Ruby could be saying.

The crowd seemed ready to kill her.

The marshals were frightened. They tried to persuade Ruby to move along. They tried to hurry her into the school, but Ruby wouldn't budge.

Then Ruby stopped talking and walked into the school.